HE DREAMS

IN ME

To include:

Have You Found Him?
He Is My Resurrection
He Wakes In Me
His Name

Neville Goddard

HE DREAMS IN ME

The Old Testament calls upon God to awake, saying: "Rouse thyself! Why sleepest thou, O Lord? Awake! Do not cast us off forever! Having hurled Himself into time/space, God is dreaming he is man and sees Himself as enslaved and cast off.

But in the New Testament, God succeeds in awakening in man, and in the *Book of Ephesians* calls upon man to "Awake and rise from the dead and Christ will give you life." Tonight, I will take the two and try to show you who this presence really is. Your own wonderful human imagination is God. It is your imagination who is calling upon you to awake, for you are all imagination and God is you and you in Him. Your external body is the imagination, and that is God Himself.

Let me begin by telling you what happened to me last Tuesday morning. Early in the morning, desiring to check the time I switched on the television to the "Today Show." Hugh Downs, the master of ceremonies, having been giving a cue to ad-lib for the next thirty seconds or so, said: "Let me tell you of a dream I once had. In the dream I was viewing a tape of one of my shows, when I said to the producer: 'Do you know, I don't remember having seen any of these people,' and the producer replied: 'That's understandable, for this show is to be taped next Friday.' When the following Friday arrived, the show I had dreamed of only a few days before was taped." In his dream, Hugh Downs merged with the future and lived an experience he did not remember.

Now, let me tell you of one who merged with the past and lived an experience of long ago. The lady writes: "I am seventy-two years old. In my dream I am a ten-year-old girl, asking my father to write in my autograph book. Having memorized a verse I wanted him to write, I dedicated it to him as he recorded it in my book. Then the dream ended.

Although I could not remember the poem prior to the dream, upon awakening I recalled every word in detail. A few days later, while visiting my daughter I told her of the dream; and when I recited the poem my daughter went to her library and - removing an old autograph book I had given her many years before - turned to the page where the verse was autographed by my third-grade teacher." Returning sixty-two years, this lady merged with a fact and remembered an experience of long ago.

The she told me of a little boy of four, who - living next door - comes to see her often. One day he told her he had always known her and that there would never be a time when they did not know each other. Describing an incident of long ago, he looked out of the window and said: "Do you see that bush? As many leaves as are on that bush are the years, and I will know you when my head grows and reaches the sky." Then one day he told her he had a dream that everything was nothing.

Modern man now concludes that the entire history of the world is laid out, and we only become aware of increasing portions of it successively. That you can merge with a section of the beginning or future relative to this moment, and experience that portion of history. How can that be? Because you are now merged with a dream.

Awakening in the morning, you think you had a wonderful dream last night; yet while you were dreaming, the experience was a reality. Awake, the dream becomes subjective. Why? Because you have once more merged with this section of time. While you are experiencing the dream, it is objective and real.

If you would only realize that the depth of your own being (which is your human imagination) is trying to instruct you, trying to persuade you, to get you aroused, as my friend's dream of the other night. Starting from the center God is working towards the surface, so it takes a while for Him to awaken and reach your surface mind. But while he is moving He is influencing your surface mind, and when He arrives you and He are no longer two, but one! You can tell when He is moving toward the surface, for He begins to question the reality of the world in which he lives.

If a lady can return and so merge with the past that she can relive an experience of long ago in detail, and a man can advance into the future and interview those who will be taped the following Friday - where is the experience of the past and where is next Friday's show? Is everything already finished and we simply tune in on certain states? Yes, for this is a dream which you can modify or radically change. In fact you are called upon to revise every day of your life and sometimes even to eradicate it.

This is a world of death and everyone here is dead, dreaming the dream of life. In the beginning we all agreed to dream in concert and no one has ever violated that agreement. There are those, however, who would not agree to this cruel experiment, as told us in the 15th chapter of the *Gospel of Luke* in the form of the parable of the prodigal son.

All through scripture you are told that God loves the second son. He loves Jacob and hates Esau. He loves Isaac and banishes Ishmael. The second son - he who enters the world of death to become a slave, hungers, awakens, and - coming to his senses - remembers the Father who gave him birth. And when he returns the Father gives him the ring, the robe, and kills that fatted calf, for "Your brother was dead and is alive. He was lost and is found." You and I, while living in this world of death are that second son, destined to awaken and remember the Father who gave us birth.

Now let me share a vision of a lady. She said: "While gazing at the fish in our pond and thinking of nothing in particular I heard a masculine voice say: 'You have run the race. You have fought the good fight.' That night as I fell asleep I heard the voice again, but this time the pronoun was changed to: 'I have run the race. I have fought the good fight. I have kept the faith.' May I tell you: having had that experience, this lady is at the end of the journey. She has kept the faith made in the beginning.

Listen to these words: "Among you stands one whom you do not know." The word translated "among" is "en" meaning "radiating from within." So, radiating from within you, stands one whom you do not know. And the word translated "stands" means "a covenant." from within you is the covenant you made with yourself, which is: you will keep the faith, and you will not turn until the race is finished. And what a race it has been!

We suffer because we are sharing in creation's cruel dream. In the beginning as the gods in scripture, we agreed to do it. As the Elohim we came down into the world of death by entering death's door, the human skull. Laying yourself down in the grave of man, you took upon yourself all of his limitations and weaknesses, and - although you will die from this section of time - there is no final death. You and I are heirs to the universe, destined to join that one being that is called the Lord.

There is not a thing you can imagine but what already is. Eternity exists. When you imagine, you claim that which already exits by identifying yourself with the state you desire to dream into objective reality. Just as the lady slipped into a section of her past and relived it as though it happened for the first time, you can slip into any section of time and live an event you desire to externalize here. We are dreaming the dream of life until we awake. So, I say, advisedly: God - your own wonderful human imagination - dreams in you.

The 44th *Psalm* is a Maskil of the Sons of Korah. The word "Maskil" means "a special, very serious instruction." The word "Korah" means "one who removes the hair on his head."[1] But the special instruction stated in the 44th *Psalm* is that which one gives to one's self: "Rouse thyself! Why sleepest thou, O Lord? Awake! Do not cast us off forever!"

Now listen to the words of Blake. Claiming that the poem, "Jerusalem" was dictated by the brothers on high, he begins it in this manner:

> *"Awake! Awake, O sleeper of the land of shadows, awake!*
> *Expand! I am in you and you in me, mutual in love divine:*
> *I am not a God afar off, I am a brother and friend;*
> *Within your bosoms I reside, and you reside in me:*
> *Lo! We are One; forgiving all Evil;*
> *Not seeking recompense!"*

Then he tells us that you and I turned away down the valleys dark, by saying: "We are not One: we are Many."

God, speaking in this great poem, calls upon man to awake, saying: "I am not a God afar off. Within your bosoms I reside and you reside in me; Lo! We are One." This I know from experience. Without loss of identity you and I are One being. We are the brothers who collectively form the Lord. Hear O Israel, the Lord our God, the Lord is one compound unity one made up of others. There is only the one Lord, who is our own wonderful human imagination. It is He who is dreaming this world in which we find ourselves.

Now let me share with you a very precious experience of a gentleman who teaches at UCLA. In his dream he encounters a teacher he has little or no respect for; but when he discovers the man to be the great examiner, his feelings change from apathy to warmth and respect.

Suddenly the exam had begun, and my friend must write his name, the date, and the hour. As he recorded his name, Monday, and the time

---

[1] *Some of our priesthoods do that today to imply that they have divine instruction which others do not possess -*

of 4:10, a thrill ran through him; and he heard a deep masculine voice say: "Not everyone who says 'Lord, Lord' enters in, but he who does the will of the Father who is in heaven."[2] When one begins to hear the words of the Father as recorded in scripture, that one is beginning to awaken from this dream of life.

In the 1st chapter of *John*, it is said that when Andrew found Jesus, he remained with him because it was the tenth hour. A day is counted from 6:00 o'clock. Broken down into three four-hour watches of the day or night, 4:00 o'clock is always the tenth hour.

Now, this is all symbolism. Ten does not mean 4:00 o'clock in the afternoon, but that moment in time when the creative power of God is being explained. The number ten whose letter "Yod" begins the name of God[3] carries the symbol of a hand, the creative hand of God. Man is separated from all other animals by reason of a hand. That which looks like a hand in the monkey or ape can convey food to the mouth but it cannot fashion, make, or create. Give a man a hand and you have a creator. You have formed in the image of his Father who is God. So here in the tenth hour the creative power of God is being revealed to my friend.

As the dream began, my friend saw the world he disliked symbolized as a person who became the great examiner to test his ability to overcome it - to modify or radically change it. And the test began at 4:10. Going over my notes, I recalled that last October, while in a dream at night, I was teaching, when I glanced at my wristwatch to discover it was 4:10 o'clock. Then I continued to explain the word of God for what appeared to be an hour or so, looked at my watch again only to find that it was still 4:10. Believing my watch had stopped, I awoke to discover it was not on my wrist, nor was it 4:10 in the morning.

Here is a vivid experience of a duplicate dream, and scripture tells us that if the dream repeats itself the thing is fixed, and the Lord will shortly bring it to pass. God's creative power is now unfolding in my friend. Now he knows his own wonderful human imagination is God. That the great I AMness in man is God and that all things are possible to Him. Now the challenge is his. Whatever he wants is! All he has to do is adjust his thinking to the state desired until it becomes alive within him, and at that moment the state will objectify itself in his world.

---

[2] *You will find this statement in the 7th chapter of the Book of Matthew -*
[3] *YOD HE VAU HE pronounced YOD HEY VAV HEY -*

A subjective desire reflected upon becomes objective. Just like the dream last night. Although subjective when you awaken and once more merge with this section of the dream, during the night it seemed the only reality.

You can take off this section of the dream, and as you merge with another, it will seem to be the only reality. The whole vast world is finished, and you and I are merged in a dream from which we are awakening.

The lady, while in a waking dream, heard the voice as she watched fish - the symbol of those who accept the gospel of salvation. Those who call upon themselves to awaken rather than call upon a god to awaken them.

So, in the Old Testament, God is called upon to "Rouse thyself! Why sleepest thou, O Lord? Awake, O sleeper and rise from the dead." God is urged to awake in the Old Testament, because God became man that man may become God, while in the New Testament the plea is for man to awake. As you test your creative power you will discover who you are. All of these acts of scripture will come to you in audible form, and you will awaken to find yourself moving into complete fulfillment of the story of Jesus Christ.

Everyone has kept the faith. No one can come down into this world and violate that agreement. You and I agreed to dream in concert before we entered death's door, the human skull. And one day we are going to awake as the poet said:

> *"He has awakened from the dream of life.*
> *'Tis we who lost in stormy visions*
> *Keep with phantoms the unprofitable strife."*

God dreams in you and you can test him any time if you are alert, for He steals into your conscious mind least disguised in the form of creative fancy. Sit down and think of a friend and watch this wonderful, moving being create mental images of him. The God of the universe is one with your wonderful human imagination.

He works in your depth, underlying all of your faculties, including perception. Then suddenly you find him moving in a serpentine manner in the form of creative fancy. When you think of someone you can catch Him; and then you will discover who God really is, for He is all within you.

Tonight, take a mere wish and see it in your mind's eye as fulfilled. Contemplate it. Merge and lose yourself completely in it. Allow your wish to take on objectivity, all the various tones of reality, so that it seems now to be the only reality. Then break it and return once more to merge in this section of your dream and reflect upon that which was so real only a moment before. Do that and no power on earth or in the universe can stop that which you have imagined from objectification.

Simply rest in confidence that it will be objectified and keep the Sabbath. The Sabbath is simply that moment when you do not make any effort to make it so, because you know it is already so! Do not labor to add to it or take from it. It is going to happen just as you judged it as good and very good.

You try it. If all things were made by God, and without Him was not anything made that was made, and you imagined and it came to pass - then you must come to the conclusion that what is done grows from what is finished. In the beginning it was only a wish, but in the end it became a fact. So, what is done grows from what is finished.

The creative power of the universe stems from imagination - the real man - for man is all imagination, and God is man and exists in us and we in Him. The eternal body of man is the imagination, and that is God Himself. Imagination is not a God afar off, but a brother and a friend.

As the Elohim we were brothers, not strangers, but - as the parable tells us - not all left our heavenly home. We ventured forth, agreeing to dream in concert or we wouldn't be here; and failure is inconceivable, for the end is simply to awaken from the eternal dream of life.

We have suffered because we are sharers in creation's cruel dream. The story is told us in the *Book of Job*. Everyone plays the part of Job. It's a crude experiment, but the end is so glorious that one forgets the pain, as told us in the 8th chapter of the *Book of Romans*: "I consider the sufferings of this present time not worth comparing to the glory to be revealed in me." We all share in the suffering, because we are dreaming in concert, dreaming the most cruel dreams; but it takes all to awaken, and in the awakening we are greater than we were prior to the beginning of the dream.

I know people see an absolute God but if God could not it would be eternal darkness. God is a creator, ever creating, ever transcending whatever He created prior to that moment when He made the commitment and entered the world of death to overcome it. That is the challenge.

Now, in the Old Testament you are calling upon God to awake, for when He awakes you are redeemed. And in the New, God did awake and is telling the world that man must awake. To no longer call upon God to awake but man, for man and God are one. God became as you are that you can become as He is. So no longer call upon a god in some remote place and time but call upon self - the one and only creative power of the world. Nothing can be created without creative power. But nothing!

If you start to imagine that things are as you desire them to be regardless of reason and your senses denial and lose yourself in that end just as though it were true, by feeling the thrill of accomplishment; and rest in confidence that it is done; and your desire projects itself on a screen of space so you can see it in your world - then you are the one they are talking about in scripture. Are you not told that by him all things were made, and without him was not anything made that was made?

And God is a person! It is a person who stands among you, not an impersonal force. Find that person and you will find him to be yourself. You are a person, and when you know what you did and see the results thereof, then you will have found him of whom Moses and the law and the prophets wrote: Jesus of Nazareth, the Son of David.

Christ is not another! Christ in you is the hope of glory! Do you not realize that Jesus Christ is in you? That's what the apostle asks in the 13th chapter of 2 *Corinthians*. Well, ask that of anyone in the world and if he is brutally honest with himself he will tell you he cannot know it until it has been experienced by him, yet here is the challenge: "Do you not realize that Jesus Christ is in you?"

Now, if Christ is the one quoted as radiating from within you, and by him all things are made and without him is not anything made that is made (even the bad), then you must find him. If there is only one maker, is it not He who made your awful day, your awful month, your awful year? If you are brutally honest with yourself, you will admit that what happened was related to your imaginal acts.

When you recognize and acknowledge this, you have found him. And because He is a person and you are a person, you know exactly who He is. Now, walk with your head up high, knowing that you have learned from your mistakes; and from now on try to imagine the best as you perceive the best to be, knowing that these acts must project themselves in this world. Then you will awaken and rejoin the brothers, for "I am not a God afar off, in me lo we are one, forgiving all evil and seeking no recognition." If we are one, why should I demand recognition? Why not forgive all, for they know not what they do.

So, I tell you: The God that you formerly dreamed in you was your own wonderful human imagination. Put him to the test. Conceive a scene implying the fulfillment of your desire and - to the best of your ability - merge with it. If you succeed in moving right into the scene, do you know it will become objective before it is seen in this section of time? It will become as objective as this world. Then when you break the spell, that which was objectively real only a moment before will be to you as a dream, but you will know it to be. Then wait in confidence that it will happen here, and when it does share it with others, that they may believe or not believe you; but tell them, because we are all one, so in the end you are simply telling yourself. That is the eternal story.

Now let us go into the silence.

HAVE YOU FOUND HIM?

Tonight's subject is: "Have you found him?" In this question I am asking if you have found the source, the cause of the phenomena of life. I can tell you from experience that he is a person as I am, as you are. Called "the Father," he is the one of whom I speak tonight.

I have met the Father. He embraced me and incorporated me into his body, so I wear[4] the human form divine, the body of infinite love. On this level this statement sounds insane, but it is true. Tonight, I am going to try to show you how he will appear when you find him.

In the wonderful poem by Robert Browning called "Saul", Saul is demented due to an evil spirit which was sent from God. David, having been anointed and made the Lord's chosen one, plays and sings to Saul, restoring him to perfect health. In the story, David prophesies the coming of the messiah, saying:

> "O Saul, it shall be
> A Face like my face that receives thee; a Man like to me,
> Thou shalt love and be loved by, forever; a Hand like this hand
> Shall throw open the gates of new life to thee! See the Christ stand!"

No one could have written this statement unless he had experienced it. But no one! Browning was raised in the environment where the matching of words and thought was an art in their practiced form and being a poet, he could tell of his experience so beautifully.

Now I will tell you mine, for I know from experience that Browning's words are true. When you see David you will see the face of the Risen Lord. If you have not seen the Risen Lord (for only the apostles see him, at which time they are incorporated into his body and sent) when you find David, use your imagination and mature his face, and you will see the face of the Risen Lord reflected there. David is the eternal youth who

---

[4] *Not to the mortal eye, but to the Spiritual eye -*

is buried in your mind, and when he comes forth and calls you Father, he will reflect your glory and bear the very stamp of your nature!

May I tell you: when I looked at David, I felt I was the Risen Lord. I am not the little garment I wear here and neither are you. In the 27th *Psalm* we are told to seek his face: "My heart says to thee, Thy face, Lord do I seek. Hide not thy face from me." I have found his face, yet I cannot take any credit for it. Having searched my entire soul I cannot find anything that I have ever done to make me worthy to behold the face of the Risen Lord; but when I was brought into his presence in the Spirit, I was incorporated into his body, into the one body, to become the one Spirit, one Lord, one God and Father of all. So, I have found him of whom Moses in the law and the prophets wrote, Jesus of Nazareth. The word "Jesus" means "Jehovah; Savior" - that's all it means - and there is only one Savior in the world. "I am the Lord your God, the Holy One of Israel, your Savior and besides me there is no Savior."

Now let me share with you a wonderful experience of a lady who is here tonight. This lady is very much a lady, yet last spring she heard a voice within her say: "You are David, my dear, and I want to love you with all of my heart." Then the voice proclaimed: "I am God and I am you!" - fulfilling the 10th chapter of *John*: "I and my Father are one," and the second *Psalm*. In this *Psalm*, David is speaking, saying: "This is the decree of the Lord: He said to me: 'You are my Son, today I have begotten you.'" This lady was called David by one who proclaimed: "I am God and I am you." I and my begotten are one!

Now, on the 24th day of May (two months after this fantastic vision) this is what she heard: "I am God himself! I am he who brings you into this world and takes you out! I AM! I AM! I AM God forever! I will never leave you. You are me, my Son, my Son, my Son! I am speaking to you from the depth of me, and I know you, Virginia. I AM! I AM Jesus Christ, your world."

In the first verse of the 43rd chapter of *Isaiah*, the Lord says: "I have redeemed you, for I have called you by name. You are mine." When you reach the point where you are called by name, you are redeemed. No matter what she must experience in the time to come, she can always lean against this experience of hers and relate it to this parallel verse of scripture. "I have redeemed you, for I have called you by name. You are mine."

May I say to all of you: if you haven't found him, don't despair. When I found him it just happened, and if it happened to me it will happen to everyone. But in this heavenly order there are certain levels, as there are in this world.

Back thirty years ago I was called into the presence of the Risen Lord, in Spirit. I was asked to name the greatest thing in the world and I answered in the words of Paul: "Faith, hope and love, these three, but the greatest of these is love." At that moment he embraced me, I was incorporated into his body, and since that time I have felt no divorce from that body. I walk the earth as Neville, the garment I shave in the morning, but at night I assume my heavenly one. While walking the earth as Neville I am just as normal as you are, yet I have never felt any estrangement from that spiritual body, for "He who is united to the Lord becomes one Spirit with him." Since that day back in 1929 I have done things you might say the Lord wouldn't do, but if anything is done the Lord had to do it, because there is nothing but God in the world!

So, in this wonderful statement of hers she was told: "Jesus Christ is your glory." Described in scripture as the power of God and the wisdom of God, Jesus Christ is your glory, and you are He! By his glorious power all things come into your world, so your world is Jesus Christ! Now, if your concept of Christ is smaller than the universe, then you don't know him, for this world in its completeness is created by and sustained by Christ. The being in the depth of this lady proclaimed the most profound thing, when she was told: "Jesus Christ is your world." He is, and he is you, for it is you who brought everything into existence.

The other day I read this little statement of James Dean, one of the greatest astrophysicists of all ages. He said: "On this planet man cannot raise his hand and not disturb the farthest star." It is here that the drama is taking place. You cannot raise an arm, you can't think, without affecting the furthest star. That's how great you are, because God became you that you may become God.

You are told in the first chapter of *John*: "In the Beginning was the Word and the Word was with God and the Word was God." The word "logos"[5] is "plan" and the plan itself is God. And "The Word became flesh and dwelt in us, and we beheld his glory, glory as the only Son from the

---

[5] *Translated "Word"* -

Father." So the Word - which is God himself - became flesh when he gave himself to you. That is the mystery of scripture. God actually became as you are, that you may be as he is!

In the Revised Standard Version of the Bible, the Greek word "en" is translated "among," but the word is "within," as in the statement: "Within you stands one whom you do not know." It is not someone who walks "among" you, but who dwells "within" you. The word "en" also means, "to give self wholly to." Emptying himself of his divinity, he took upon himself the form of a slave and became the obedient unto death, even death upon this physical cross of man. The body you wear is the cross upon which God is crucified, and from which God will rise, taking you with him. Then you will know that you and he are one.

I was sent to tell you the true story of the mystery of Christ. While we are here on this inferior level of awareness, we have lost sight of our maker, but I have been sent to tell you how the drama of Christ unfolds within you, as it is the Father's will that not one be lost, not one in my holy mountain.

Paul tells us in his letter to the *Corinthians* that, like in the army, there are various levels of awareness. He puts the apostles first, the prophets second, the teachers third, and the miracle workers fourth. Why he does this I do not know. I do know that I used the words of Paul when the Risen Christ asked me to tell him what was the greatest thing in the world, and after he embraced me and I fused with his body, I was sent with the words: "Down with the bluebloods."

People may think this has something to do with the social order, but the word means "church protocol; the traditions of men, as opposed to the commands of God." The world is full of the traditions of men, which change as fast as they are created. Wanting to sell more fish, tradition dictated that it was a sin to eat meat on Friday. Now that tradition has changed, and you are allowed to eat meat on Friday once more. The early fathers were all married; then one came along who was ignorant and wanted everyone to be as ignorant as he, so he made an order that they marry no more. Now the men are rebelling and it will only take a few years before it will all be back to the way it was. These are the traditions of men, while I was sent to fulfill the command of God.

Christianity hasn't a thing to do with that which is made by the human hand. The "church" of scripture is "the assembly of the resurrected." The resurrected are those who are incorporated into the body of the Risen Christ, and - may I tell you - it is a body just as real as yours is now. Everyone will be incorporated into that one body, yet there are orders there just as there are here in this physical body. The eyes perform a function, the ear another, the nose another, as each perform their own special function.

Paul takes eight (which is the number of Christ) and gives eight orders within the body, but what determines this order I do not know. I only know that I beheld his face, he embraced me and incorporated me into his body, and when I found David he was simply a young impression of the Ancient of Days I had beheld.

That is why Browning made David say:

> *"O Saul it shall be*
> *A Face like my face that receives thee; a Man like to me,*
> *Thou shalt love and be loved by, forever; a Hand like this hand*
> *Shall throw open the gates of new life to thee! See the Christ stand!"*

And you know, you cannot earn this experience. It is all grace, grace, and more grace. So begin now to live a wonderful life and exercise your imagination lovingly on behalf of everyone. And one day you will be called to enter that one body, and it will not matter whether you play the part of the teacher, the miracle worker, the helper, the administrator, or the speaker in tongues. If one is playing the part of the apostle, it is not because he earned it. It's a play, and the part he is playing was God's choice in the beginning, before that the world was.

So, learn to exercise your creative power by applying the law, for you may have anything you want! You want to be wealthy, you may have it. You want to be known, you may have that too. Anything you want you may have, but when it comes to God's promise - it will be fulfilled. It is my hope that it is now, but don't think you can make it happen - you can't. But you will find Him when you see David and he calls you Father; and he will, for there is only one God and Father of us all who is above all, through all, and in all.

In the meantime, remember: everything is a state of consciousness. You want security? Then assume that you are secure, and things will happen and you will bear the fruit of the tree of security. Get out of that state, and its fruit will vanish. You may wonder what happened and think someone deceived you - the market went down or your product is no longer wanted - but you can only eat the fruit of security when you know you are its tree. Any state occupied bears its fruit, and your world is forever bearing witness to the state you are in. But you will never find the cause of the phenomena of life until the David of Biblical fame (who is my son) calls you Father, and then and only then, will you know that you and I are one.

Now let us go into the silence.

HE IS MY RESURRECTION

The gospel, which appears to be a little secular story, is truly a mystery to be known only by revelation.

In the 16th chapter of *John* we are told: "I came out from the Father and came into the world. Again, I leave the world and I return to the Father." In these four short phrases we find the pre-existence of Christ, his incarnation, his death, and his ascension. I could put this in the first person, plural sense and say: "We came out from the Father" for we are told in the 1st chapter of *Ephesians*: "He chose us in him before the foundation of the world." So, all of us were chosen in him. That is why I can say, "We came out from the Father and came into the world. Again, we are leaving the world and are going to the Father."

How can this be? Let me use a simple analogy. A plant contains within itself the suckers which can be removed and transplanted. While existing within the plant, the suckers partake of the plant's life, but when removed and transplanted they become the parent.

It was God's purpose to give us himself, and God is a Father. The only way he could do it however was to detach us from himself. Yet, like the sucker, he who sent us has never left us; therefore, we must express that which the parent plant is. If its flowers were red, that which was transplanted will bear red flowers. Now, regardless of how healthy the stock may be, when it is transplanted it appears to die, showing us the secret of life through death. The seed falls into the ground and dies in order to be made alive. So the seed, containing within itself all that the parent contained, dies and is made alive to become the parent, containing within itself that which was in the parent stock.

And so it is with us. We came out from God the Father and were planted in a world of death, a world of mortality. Then, having died, we become quickened and grow into the parent stock, for if we were a father before detachment, we must return as the one Father who sent us out. And everything God the Father possesses, we possess in our fullness. His son reveals himself as our son. Whatever happened to him happens to us, for we came out from the Father and came into the world. Again, as we leave the world we go to the Father. That is the great mystery of scripture.

Let me now tell you of a vision a lady who is here tonight shared with me. She found herself viewing a very long train ascending from a very dark cavern into which she descended. Immediately upon entering its blackness, she imagined herself aboard the train and was instantly on it. Moving up at an incredible speed, she wondered about her destiny, when a voice said: "It will not be long," and she entered a world filled with pinnacles and sparkling light. Then a triangular-shaped light penetrated her brain and she found herself standing in front of a very tall chair upon which a great being was seated. As she gazed into his eyes she felt herself immersed in love and in a voice so very tender he called her, "Babe." Feeling so small and young among these pinnacles, she said: "What shall I do?" when something exploded in her and she heard a voice and saw the words, "Record It" appear in script before her eyes. Seeing me in the distance, she said: "That is Neville" and the being seated in the chair began to describe me in the most endearing, possessing terms ending with these words: "He is my resurrection." This statement was picked up by invisible voices which echoed and re-echoed and re-echoed all the way down through time as she awoke.

Yes, she saw the Father. I am his resurrection. He buried himself in me as he buried himself in you before you came out from him. Having resurrected the Father in me, I am his resurrection and know myself to be the Father. Before coming out I did not know this. I partook of the tree of life, but I was not individualized.

There never was a time that you and I were not partaking of this tree of life, but we were not individualized. We did not voluntarily detach ourselves and enter this world, but were made subject unto futility in the hope that we would be set free from this body of death and obtain the glorious liberty of the sons of God. Now, the Son of God is one with God, for the son erupts into the Father. Like the sucker which contains within itself everything that the parent tree contains, but cannot know it until detached and transplanted, we contain within ourselves everything the tree of life contains, but will not know it until we come out from the Father and come into the world. Having died, death will be transformed into sleep, from which we will all awaken as God the Father. Individually we will all have these four mighty acts erupt from within to spell out the being we really are.

In the statement: "I came out from the Father" the pre-existence of Christ in you, who is your hope of glory, is established. I am not speaking of some little man who walked the earth 2,000 years ago, but of the mystery of Christ which is buried in every child born of woman. Christ, God's creative power and wisdom, pre-existed. His detachment and entrance into the world through his birth from below is his birth into death. Then, after the long interval of death he is born from above into a world of life. Having come out from the Father and coming into the world, his return to the Father is essential. He comes back bearing witness to the fullness within himself of all that the parent contained, thereby knowing he is the Father. This is how all the fathers return.

We are told that in the last days scoffers will come, saying: "Where is the promise of his coming? Forever since the fathers fell asleep, all things have continued as they were from the beginning of creation." The scoffers do not know that a thousand years is as a day to the Lord; therefore, six days would be like 6,000 years to mortal eye. As He promised, you will return on time, not a moment before or after.

Your return begins through the impregnation by one who has awakened. He does not arbitrarily choose his offspring. They are called by the depth of his own being. But he is spiritually born to play the part of siring that section of time to which he belongs, a role he did not choose but was born to play.

Now let me tell you of another vision. This lady said: "While standing at attention in a military drill, Marta and I were called to the front where you, Neville, dressed in a long black robe, presented us each with a black umbrella, which was opened and raised over our heads. Then you spoke profound words of eternal wisdom.

"Suddenly the scene changed and Marta and I, still with the umbrellas over our heads, are standing in a room, when I said to Marta: 'Did you understand what he said?' and she answered: 'No.' Dorothy Dix then entered the room and said: 'I will explain it to you.' I was so surprised with that remark that I awoke."

The symbolism in this vision was perfect: a black robe and black umbrellas. In symbolism, black is the incomprehensible divine silence, eternity. In the Song of Solomon, the bride speaks, saying: "I am black."

The word translated "black" should be "the blackest of black." In Hebrew there are no superlatives or comparative. To emphasize the comparative, a word must be repeated, as "black-black." To make it superlative, the word must be repeated three times, such as "holy, holy, holy," as there is no way to say "holiest" in Hebrew. The world "black" spoken by the bride should be repeated to the nth degree. "I am black, but comely O daughters of Jerusalem, black like the curtains of Solomon." Here, black is the incomprehensible mystery, and in her dream she did not understand it. Then one appears who she least expected to be able to interpret it, but one who was present, by invitation, at the last supper. Don't discount that.

Now, this vision was preceded by a conversation following my last lecture, when this lady, knowing she had been impregnated by the Holy Spirit, said to her friend: "What am I going to do for the next thirty years?" And her friend replied: "What are you talking about? Did he not tell you that you are blessed? What's thirty years when you have been waiting throughout eternity to reach this point in time? How can you be concerned, when you know that in just thirty years you will depart this world and enter an entirely different age?" That conversation prompted the vision which she did not understand, because I was dressed in black as I revealed the mystery of mysteries. "I am black, but comely O daughters of Jerusalem, black as the curtains of Solomon." This is the blackest of black, containing divine silence, eternity, and an incomprehensible secret which Dorothy knew (but don't forget: Dorothy was present by invitation to the last supper).

Another lady who is here tonight shared this experience with me, saying: "In my dream I was talking to two people, when one looked at me and said: 'How far is it?' to which I replied: 'It is only thirty minutes away' and awoke."

This lady has conceived of the Holy Spirit and is now waiting - not minutes, miles, or hours, but thirty years for the child to be born. Again I will say: what does it matter? She told me that all through her life she has never wanted things and knows that is why she has never accumulated worldly possessions. Hers has been a questing mind, always seeking, always searching for the cause of life. May I tell her that at this moment she is richer than the richest man in the world, for she has been selected to receive the imprint, receive the gift of God Himself.

We came out from the Father, containing within ourselves the ovum (all that is necessary to become the Father). Walking through the centuries we have carried our egg, awaiting that moment in time when the egg is fertilized. One who is a Son of God by nature, having been born for that purpose, will be used in that capacity so that others may become sons of God by grace. It is all supernaturally done. Some remember when the union took place, but it is not experienced on this level at all.

In the meanwhile, don't neglect the law of God which is: An assumption will harden into fact. If an assumption creates its own reality then there is no such thing as fiction. I may forget what I assumed today and when it appears I may not recognize my own harvest, but it could not enter my world had I not brought it in by an imaginal act.

Tonight, some unknown author is writing a story in order to pay the rent. The story may not sell, but for a moment he will lose himself in its creation, and when his story comes to pass in the tomorrows, those whose lives will be touched will not recognize his harvest. Tonight, the movie, "A Night to Remember" will be shown on television. Although the movie was recently made, it is based upon the sinking of the Titanic in 1912, which duplicated a book called Futility, written in 1898. In the novel, a ship filled with the rich and complacent was on its maiden voyage, when it sank on an iceberg in the Atlantic. Fourteen years later the White Star Line built a duplicate of the imaginary ship described in the book, filled it with the rich and complacent, where it sank on its maiden voyage on an iceberg in the Atlantic. And people say there is fiction? No, there is no fiction.

There is not a moment in time when imagination is not acting, causing the events of the world. You may not remember your thoughts and deny you have anything to do with what you are reaping, but you can only harvest what you plant. Kennedy's death was a violent action, but I am told that the Kennedys had apparently felt they were destined to lose their sons this way. As a family they entertained this sense of martyrdom, this sense of violence which caused it to come to pass. There are no accidents; as a man sows, he reaps. You are free as the wind to imagine anything, but you must be willing to pay the price, for you will reap the results. Imagining yourself to be a good author you can write a horrible story of hate and violence and reap the results, for the hate you write about goes out and brings the violence back into your own being.

A friend recently told me that when he was about nine years old he received a Ouija board. One day he asked the board: "Who am I" and it spelled out the word "Christ." Believing the board completely, he thought he was Jesus reincarnated, but when he told his minister (who was of the high church of the Episcopal world) he was immediately educated out of what they called "neurotic sin." Believing he had sinned because of entertaining the thought, he prayed for a great sacrament and complete absolution of this sin, when a marvelous vision descended upon him revealing an altar with everything attached.

These so-called "wise" people, who go around with their long robes and conduct a service in Latin which no one understands, should read scripture. Paul said: "I would rather speak five words that can be understood than ten thousand words in an unknown tongue." If you want to speak Latin go to the Vatican, but don't come here where very few people understand one word outside of English (and even that poorly) and speak in an unknown tongue. Speak the tongue in which you were born that you may be understood or be silent.

This lad was educated out of his belief when he should have continued in it, as Christ in him is his hope of glory. Scripture urges you to examine yourself, to test yourself and see if Jesus Christ is now in you. And if all things are made by him and without him is not a thing made that is made, who is he? I'll tell you who he is. He is your own wonderful human imagination. How do I know this to be true? By imagining a state, remaining faithful to it and watching it come to pass in my world. Believing that God makes all things, I made my desired state alive and can now trace its maker back to my imagination.

Now I know that Man is all Imagination, and God is Man and exists in us and we in Him. The Eternal Body of Man is the Imagination and that is Jesus, the divine body of which we are His members. I know this because if He makes all things and I imagine, remain faithful to my imaginal state and it happens. I have found him, not as someone divorced from me, but as my own wonderful human imagination.

So that little planchette, moved by this lad's own unconscious motion, revealed his true identity; yet the so-called wise men called it neurotic sin. I know exactly what he went through, for I was raised in the low church of the Episcopal world and my mother used to tell me that the priests were the wisest men in the world. I believed her until I became a man and the visions began to appear within me. Then I realized how very stupid they really are. Throughout the centuries they have fooled the people into believing they are so wise because they can speak a little phrase in Latin. But when you ask them to explain the verse I spoke of tonight: "I came out from the Father and came into the world, again I am leaving the world and going to the Father" they give you only the literal meaning and say that a glorious being came out from the Father.

"Where?" you ask, and they reply: "Don't ask questions, my son."

"He came out in what way?"

"Out of our holy blessed mother."

"In what manner did he do it?"

Again, "Don't ask questions, my son. This is the great secret of the church."

At the end of your conversation you will discover you have been talking to one who doesn't know the answers, so he gives you all kinds of confused thoughts to bewilder you. During my thirty years on the platform I have talked with them time and time again. They stand open-mouthed and bewildered as I speak from experience, while they speak from theory. They call it blasphemy when I tell them I have found the Son of God who called me Father, yet I see them as blind leaders of the blind, as foretold in scripture.

I tell you: your own wonderful human imagination is Jesus Christ. There never was another and there never will be another. One day He will awaken in you and all that is said of him will be experienced by you in the first person present tense; and may I tell you: far from being ashamed, you will be thrilled beyond measure. All you have ever done as a man in this world of mortality of which you are ashamed will be wiped clean. It is necessary for you to go through the muck and mire of this world so that this seed may erupt. And when it does you are one with God, who is perfect, and your entire past is wiped out as though it never were.

There is no such thing as earning your way into heaven. Heaven is not earned; it is a gift. When you hear salvation's story and believe it, the kingdom will unveil itself from within, and from that moment on no man, regardless of his position in the secular world, can stand before you and make you feel unimportant. You will simply ignore his words, knowing that although he may sit on a throne he does not know who he is. And tomorrow if he leaves this world he will find himself in a world just like this, in an environment best suited for the work yet to be done in him, while you - unknown by the world - will instantly possess your immortal garment and mortality will be blotted out by light.

In the 5th chapter of 2 *Corinthians*, Paul is speaking to those he addressed when he said: "We groan in this body waiting for our heavenly body," as he was hoping spiritual birth would come to them before death appears. Death here in the twenty-eighth year would leave you still unclothed in a spiritual sense, as you would still have two more years to go to be clothed with immortality. A lady here tonight is not yet twenty-eight, but her memory returned to another age, another time, and she said: "I recall you vividly. You haven't changed. You still have the same face, the same voice. You told me than about a father and a son and I didn't understand."

I tell you: throughout the night I move through sections of time, for I have other sheep that are not of this body. I must gather them all into one fold before I can return to the Father as the Father. This is my story.

You dwell upon it and don't neglect the principle of your wonderful imagination. Use it lovingly on behalf of everything, for when you do, you are using it on yourself, as there is no other. The world is yourself pushed out. Imagine and then drop it. You don't have to burst a blood vessel, call the "right" people, or do the "right" thing in order to succeed. All you need do is assume you are now what you want to be. Remain faithful to that assumption and in a way that no one knows you will become it. Then try it again and again, and while you are about your Father's business working this principle, another work, unknown to the world, is taking place in you, preparing you for the fullness of time when the egg you have been carrying throughout the centuries is fertilized. Then, thirty years later, it erupts and all that is said of Christ is experienced in a personal, most intimate manner.

Now let us go into the silence.

HE WAKES IN ME

Tonight's subject is "He Wakes in Me". I should say "he wakes in us". Who is he? The Lord Jesus Christ who is crucified in us. He was never crucified on anything outside of man, and because he was crucified in us, he must rise in us. Paul said: "I have been crucified with Christ; it is not I who live, but Christ who lives in me. And if we have been united with him in a death like his we shall certainly be united with him in a resurrection like his."

The resurrection, although not described in any portion of scripture, is really the high watermark, the very center of the Christian faith. As Paul said: "If Christ is not raised then our faith is in vain and we are as men the most to be pitied."

Sunday morning the churches are going to proclaim that Christ is risen, and they should, because Christ is risen - but how do we know this? By the witnesses! By those who have experienced the resurrection. The experience of the resurrection in the lives of the apostles is the indispensable inner testimony without which Jesus Christ might have been raised, but could not have been preached as risen. Everyone who is called, who experiences the resurrection, who experiences Christianity in its fullness, is an apostle, for you cannot experience it and not see the Risen Christ. Coming from within everyone will be raised, one by one, to unite into one single body, one Spirit, one Lord, one God and Father of us all. There is only one.

We are told in scripture that our lowly bodies will be changed to be of one form with his glorious body. Not like it, but of one form with it. There is only one form, one body, one Spirit, one hope, one Lord, one faith, one baptism, one God and Father of us all who is above all, through all, and in all. And in the 8th chapter of *Mark* it is said: "Those who are ashamed of my words, of him the Son of man will be ashamed when he comes into the glory of his Father with the heavenly angels." These words precede the resurrection. In fact, when the drama is coming to its close, these events - although separated in time - are but part of a single complex. Now let me share one of these with you.

In 1946, I felt myself lifted up as I heard a heavenly chorus sing my praise and my victory over death. I felt as though I were a being of fire, clothed in a body of air. The body was self-luminous, as told in the 9th chapter of *Mark*: "His garments radiated light with such an intensity that no fuller on earth could bleach a garment comparable to it." The garment was not white, but radiant light. There was no need for any external light, no sun, no moon, no stars, for I was light enough. I could see as far as vision desired, and as I glided by a sea of human imperfection, everyone was made perfect. Eyes returned to the empty sockets of the blind, the missing arms returned, the lame walked. Every conceivable imperfection vanished as I glided by, accompanied by this wonderful, heavenly chorus singing my praises and calling me by name. When the last one was made perfect, the chorus sang out: "It is finished" (which is the last cry on the cross) and I felt myself - now a being of fire clothed in a garment of air - actually crystallize into this tiny little body called Neville. I felt so bound, so restricted, as though I couldn't turn in any direction.

On this level your body is animated and wonderful, but you cannot compare it to that radiant garment which is your transfigured self. You will wear this heavenly garment before you experience the resurrection, yet this is the garment of the Risen Christ. There is no other garment of Christ and there is only one Christ, so everyone who is raised is he. We are told in Paul's letter to the *Corinthians* (I think it is the 6th chapter): "God raised the Lord and we also shall be raised by his power", and may I tell you: what a power! Called the power of God, it comes to you just like a wind. At first you feel it as a vibration, but when it hits you, this transfigured self is a wind, an unearthly wind.

Then in 1959 the resurrection came, followed by my birth into an entirely new age. The resurrection begins the entire drama of Christianity, although many experiences precede it, as you wear your transfigured self and know yourself to be a being of fire dwelling in a body of air. The resurrection comes so suddenly. There is no warning, for in this transfigured state you are told to tell no one until the Son of man is raised from the dead.

Man has been taught to believe that a man was crucified on a wooden tree, taken down from it, and put into a grave - and it isn't so at all! Christ, the great Messiah, is buried in you as your creative power and wisdom, which is God's creative power and wisdom lowered to this level. Buried in you, it dreams horrible experiences; but in the end this power begins to stir and as it does, it fulfills all that was foretold in scripture regarding itself.

Now listen to the words of Moses (the eternal state of the prophet through which all men pass) as recorded in the *Book of Deuteronomy*: "The Lord, your God will raise up for you a prophet like me from among you, from your brethren – him you shall heed." Do not read this passage on the surface because translations are strange. Go back to find the Hebrew meaning for every word in the sentence. We will take just the one word, translated in the Revised Standard Version as "among" and in the King James Version as "midst". The Hebrew word thus translated means: "Within yourself; the heart; the bowel; the very core of a person; the inmost thought of man." So, "From within you the Lord God will raise up for you a prophet like me."

Moses was the one in the ancient world who experienced the transfiguration. And when he returned to the Israelites, his body shone so, that he had to cover it, for they could not behold the glory of the man. Here is the prototype of the one who is to be raised up out of man, from man. Something comes out of man that is the Lord, the Messiah, the Lord Jesus Christ. It's not something that comes out and leaves you here. Your garment is the grave in which God is buried as your own wonderful human imagination.

Everything in your world is produced by imagination. There isn't a thing that was not first imagined, yet when it becomes an objective fact it seems so independent of your perception of it, that you forget its origin and do not realize it was produced by you. Everything that appears without was first an image, nothing more than a dream which was created by the dreamer in you, who is the Lord Jesus Christ.

Then one day your imagination begins to stir and without warning you are resurrected. This is how it happened to me. I retired as usual, just as I have done throughout the years. Then came this unearthly wind.[6] Intensifying itself in my head, I felt as though I was going to explode, that I must be experiencing a massive hemorrhage. But instead I began to awake to discover I was in my skull. I was more awake than I had ever

---

[6] *In both Hebrew and Greek the word "spirit" and "wind" are the same, so when you speak of the Spirit of the Lord you speak of the wind -*

been before. I knew a clarity of thought I had never known before, yet I was entombed in my skull and it was completely sealed.

Standing alone in this empty tomb, I was consumed with the desire to get out. Possessing a peculiar, innate knowledge, as though built in at the beginning of time, I knew that if I pushed the base of my skull something would move. Obeying that instinct I pushed, and something rolled away leaving an opening large enough for me to put my head through. Then I squeezed myself out inch by inch, just like a child coming out of the womb of a woman. For a few seconds I remained on the floor, and then rose to look at this body out of which I had come. It appeared to be dead, but its head was moving from side to side.

As I looked, I realized I had been in that body all this time and had not realized it was a tomb. I had always thought that it was I. If someone struck my hand they struck me! If food was placed in my mouth I ate it. If the body was fed, bathed, or shaved, it was me for as far as I was concerned I am it. It never occurred to me that the body was a garment I was wearing and it was a garment of death.

Then the wind increased, but instead of being in my head it was coming from the corner of the room, causing me to divert my attention from the garment on the bed. When I looked again, the garment was gone and in its place were my three brothers, one sitting at the head, and the other two where the feet were. They, too, heard the wind, for one rose and as he walked towards it his attention was attracted to something on the floor, and before he even picked it up he said: "It's Neville's baby." The other two, in incredulous voices, said: "How can Neville have a baby?" He didn't argue the point, but simply produced the evidence: an infant wrapped in swaddling clothes.

Now, I didn't give birth to a child; the child is but a sign. Scripture tells us: "This shall be a sign unto you. You shall find a babe wrapped in swaddling clothes." The babe is a sign that God is born. That his power is born on a higher level of his own being. God buried himself and then raised himself, and the evidence that he rose is called a birth, of which a child is the symbol. A little babe wrapped in swaddling clothes is a sign unto you that Spirit was born, for flesh and blood cannot inherit the kingdom of heaven, neither can the perishable inherit the imperishable. If you are to enter the kingdom, you must leave the garment of flesh and blood which you have been wearing throughout the centuries.

So, the resurrection is followed by your birth from above. Then come all the other events, which stretch over a period of 3½ years as told us in scripture. "When Jesus began his ministry, he was thirty years of age, and his ministry lasted 3½ years." It is exactly 1260 days, or 3½ years, to the end of the great drama. Then, as told us in the *Book of Acts*,[7] you will remain in the world because the need is great to persuade others of the kingdom of God and of the truth concerning Jesus Christ, and some will be persuaded by what you say, while others will disbelieve.

Then you will depart this world never to return again, for you will have raised yourself to a higher power and know yourself to be the one God and Father of all.

There are not many Christ's running around. Not many Messiahs, only one. We are all united into that one body, one Spirit, one hope, one Lord, one faith, one baptism, one God and Father of us all. The word "Jesus" and the word "Jehovah" mean "Jehovah saves" or "Jehovah is salvation" and the only savior recorded in scripture is the Lord. "I am the Lord your God the Holy One of Israel, your Savior and besides me there is no savior." Where is he? Crucified within you. Having limited himself to man by assuming the state of death, God transcends the limitation of this little garment and overcomes death.

Everything in this world waxes, wanes, and vanishes. There is nothing here that is eternal, nothing immortal. We speak of someone having immortality in his architecture or his music, but that is nonsense. This is a world of death where even the most concrete mountain decays. But there is something buried in man that is immortal, destined to overcome his self-imposed limitation. And when he rises in you, you are the one who is rising. And when the union takes place, it is not another. Without loss of identity you will wear the garment of the Risen Christ. Without loss of identity every child born of woman will wear the one garment of the Risen Christ.

Don't ask me to explain the mystery of how one can contain all, but it does. You might just as well as ask how your body can contain billions of cells, or your brain billions of atoms - I don't know. How can I say that my own loins contain as many children as I am capable of siring? They

---

[7] *Now in the form of one called Paul -*

all come from me, yet they seem to be many bodies when they enter this world; but in the end they will all be gathered back into the one body.

Now a fragmented one, when you are regathered into the one body you are far greater than you were prior to the fragmentation, for truth is an ever increasing illumination. There is no such thing as ultimate truth. If that were true it would be stagnation. Truth is forever increasing, and so is power and so is wisdom.

God buried his creative seed in you and as it begins to awaken you are transformed in consciousness. As we are told in *Philippians*: "He will change my lowly body to be of one form with his glorious body." This is done when Christ is formed in you. Your lowly body is transformed to be of one form with his glorious body, for as he is formed in you he is your very self. And when you are raised from the dead you must be he, for only the Lord is raised. You are told: "God raised the Lord, and we are born anew through the resurrection of Jesus Christ within us." If Jesus Christ is within, and I am born anew through his resurrection, and I do not see another but know I resurrected, then I have found him - not as another, but as my own wonderful human imagination. Now put him to the test.

Let me give you something tonight to put your mental teeth into. A friend of mine who is here tonight told me of an experience he had in a dream. He was an actor, playing the part and wearing the costume of a Greek. In the scene he was to be shot, and the actor who was to shoot him was told to use a blank, but this night the bullet was real. As he fell to the floor, he rose from that body, completely restored to life and said: "Why that S.O.B. – he shot me!" Then he awoke.

Last week Milton Berle's nephew, a fine young lad in his twenties, was simulating the catching of a car thief. (It was a drama, too, for it was not an actual event). The deputy didn't know his gun was loaded, but as Berle - now playing the part of the thief - began to run as directed, the deputy pulled his gun and shot him.

Now, if it would give the boy's family any comfort, I would tell them that their son has experienced the resurrection. He has experienced the birth from above. He has experienced the Fatherhood of God by the discovery of the only begotten Son, David, who calls him Father, and is now waiting for the final curtain - in the form of a dove - to descend. I say this, for if the taking of innocent blood results in redemption (as it does in my friend's case), then the killing of young Berle also results in redemption.

If one could only see that everything in this world is moving for good because God planned it all. "As I have planned, so shall it be, and as I have purposed, so shall it stand. I will not turn back until all that I have planned is perfectly fulfilled." That's what we are told in scripture. And all things work for good to those who love the Lord, and I am quite sure the young boy attended some form of synagogue or church and there was a measure of love there.

If one goes into battle to kill and be killed, that's not innocent blood. But when someone innocently walks by - perhaps in a protest march - and someone kills him, his is innocent blood. He had no intention of killing anyone but walked unarmed when shot. Now, what a blessing this seeming disaster would be if this innocent blood results in redemption, which is a complete lifting up and raising oneself from this wheel of recurrence, this eternal death!

So, I tell you: The Lord Jesus Christ wakes in you, and when he wakes, you are he, for in the end there is Jesus only. Climbing the mountain, you see Moses - the prototype of the law, and Elijah - the prototype of the promise. But when you return from the mountaintop, now fully awake, the prototype of both the law and the promise have vanished, and you walk knowing yourself to be the embodiment and fulfillment of all law and prophecy; so in the end there is Jesus only, and you are he.

There is nothing but Jesus, who is Jehovah. It is he who is playing all the parts, for there is nothing but God. So, in the end everyone will awake, for everyone is that being who is the Elohim, the compound unity of one made up of others. We are the gods who agreed to the unity of dreaming in concert. That's the oneness. Here is the dreamer, the assemblage of the gods in perfect agreement. In one consciousness we agree to the play and become fragmented, but only the one God is playing all the parts. You say, "I am" before you say anything and I say, "I am" before I say "Neville". If your name is *John*, before you say, "John" you say, "I am." That's the name of God. He has no other name.

You can't divide I am, yet you do see it fragmented when you see another. You may look at a fragmentation, but you cannot divide I am. How can you? "Go and tell them that I am is my name forever. This is the name by which I shall be known throughout all generations." You can't divide it! You may ask a question and a seeming other may answer, but their reply comes from a source who says, "I am" Grace, "I am" Jan, "I am" Paul, or "I am" Bill. All responses precede the mask they wear by saying "I am", so in the end there is only one God, only One, nothing but God!

This wonderful story is true. I am speaking, not from hearsay or speculation. I am not theorizing but telling you what I know from experience. I am like Paul; I must remain and tell it because of the need, and I tell it from morning 'till night, and some will believe while others disbelieve. But when I go, those who believe will continue the message and the others will eventually believe. No one will be lost, for in the end everyone will be redeemed, because if one is gone, the whole is not put together. There will be a missing part in the puzzle, and no one worthy of the name of God would leave a piece out. He can't push it in; he has to make it fit as it ought to. Everything has to fit, for in the beginning was a plan and in the end the plan will be fulfilled. All will awaken to the knowledge that they are God. There is nothing but God.

But no one can become conscious on the higher level by any good work that he does. You can't earn it. There is no such thing as accumulating merit; it's simply "God raised the Lord and will also raise us by his power." Each in his own good time. We are all gathered together, one after the other, but each in his own good time. There is a plan to the entire thing, and the will of the Lord will not turn back until he has executed and accomplished the intents of his mind. "In the latter days"[8] "you will understand it perfectly." You will see how everything was done according to a definite plan.

Now let us go into the silence.

---

[8] *As told us in the Book of Jeremiah -*

HIS NAME

The Bible is not a product of human beings; it is not constructed by man. It is the history of man's discovery by God's revelation of the changing name of God, and it increases in its value to man. In *Genesis* 4:26 we are told that a child was born whose name was Enosh, born to Sarah, and men began to call upon the name of the Lord. That is the first time that man began to call upon the name of the Lord. The word Enosh means "mortal man," something that is fragile, something that simply wears out and disappears. Mortal man began to ask concerning his origin: Why am I here, what is the cause of the phenomena of life?

The next time we see it is in the 32nd chapter of *Genesis*. This is the night, we are told, a man called Jacob (the supplanter) wrestled with God, and when it came to the breaking of the day God said to him: "Let me depart." And he said: "I will not let you depart until you bless me." And God blessed him. Then he said to God: "What is your name?" and God answered: "Why do you ask my name?" He would not tell him, so Jacob called the spot where God touched him "Peniel," which means "the face of God," for said he "I have seen God face to face and yet my life is preserved." Then as the sun rose Jacob faltered because where God had touched shrank. It was the sinew upon his thigh. That is what man at that level of consciousness believed to be the creative power of the universe.

Today, 1963, you and I are witnesses to the most fantastic things that man has conceived. Missiles in space that can reach the sun, these IBM machines, electronic brain - but nothing that man has ever devised or brought to birth can compare to a child. Nothing in this world that man can conceive is comparable to the brain of a child. For the child conceived the instrument that now frightens us. We have a bomb, nuclear bomb, but that can't compare to the brain that conceived it, no matter what we do with it. Read *Genesis 32*, where man once thought the sex act was God. The very act of producing the most sensitive thing in the world is the form of a child. (There isn't a part of the world that someone hasn't erected phallic images in its worship of God.)

Now we turn to the *Book of Exodus,* where the name changes because it wasn't yet revealed. Man began to call upon the name of the Lord, but they didn't know what to call upon; they thought it was sex. Read Exodus 3:13-15, how God reveals himself to his chosen vessel, Moses. And Moses said to the Lord: "When I come to the people of Israel and I say to them, 'the Lord, your God, has sent me unto you,' and they ask me 'What is his name?' what shall I say? And the Lord answered: "I AM who I AM." The words are every form of the verb "to be" - "I AM that I AM" - I will be what I will be. "Say unto them, 'I AM has sent me unto you.'" So, when you come to the people of Israel, say to them the God of your father, the God of Abraham, the God of Isaac and the God of Jacob has sent me unto you, and this is my name forever: "I AM." No other. And this will lead you out of the wilderness into the promised land. That was the second grand revelation of the name of God. Man thought it was the creative act. Who could deny that nothing in this world that man has ever created was comparable to that of a child - nothing. And he has to trace it back to his origin of the act, and all of a sudden it came out of this fantastic organism. And then comes a revelation of another kind, that the name is "I AM."

Then comes the final revelation, which we find in the New Testament, and he brings something entirely different that man has not seen before. He reveals the name as "Father." "Holy Father, keep them in thy name which thou hast given unto me, that they may be one as you and I are one." He gave them the name that was his name and the name was 'Father" - the final revelation of God to man concerning who he really is, his father. "So, in many and various ways God spoke of old to our fathers by the prophets but in these last days he has spoken to us by a son." If he has spoken by a son, then he is a father. And so God speaks to man in his final days through his son, and the son reveals to that man that he is the father of that son, and then - and only then, does man know who he really is. But until that day comes take the second revelation of the name of God, which is "I AM" and use it and use it wisely. You can use it for anything in the world. You are told if you blaspheme against his name you must be stoned to death, as told us in *Leviticus 24:16*: "Anyone who blasphemes against the name I AM," and the name has already been revealed in *Leviticus 3*. *Exodus 2* revealed the name. Now if you blaspheme against this name, stone him to death.

One who was born of a Hebrew woman who knew an Egyptian man, cursed the name of God, and they listened to see what God would say to do to such a man: stone him to death. Stone does not mean that you take stones and throw at him, as people will do. The stones are the literal facts of life. How could I blaspheme against the name of God? With God all things are possible, so his name is "I AM." And I dare to say: "I am unwanted; I am poor; I am ill; I am completely ignored in this world." Well, this is blasphemy against God. For it is not what I really want in this world, or for anyone else that I love. So here I am blaspheming against God.

I am told in *John 8*: "Except you believe that I am he you shall die in your sins." "Sin" is missing the mark. If I don't believe that I am the man I want to be, I remain where I am at that moment of not daring to assume that I am the man that I want to be, and remain in that limitation, so I die, missing the mark. So, the being you really are - if the second revelation is true (and I can tell you it is true, that his name is "I AM") - it doesn't mean you worship something on the outside when you say, "I am." And the day that you actually contact it as though the "I-thou" concept was within yourself, you feel who you really are.

Now here is a true story which I heard this last Saturday. I am not a member of the Turf Club, but I go occasionally when I am invited and someone takes me. So last Saturday I and my wife were taken to the Turf Club. I was introduced to this little man who sat just one row below. Strange, weird little fellow, and then they told me his story. He had come here penniless from Kentucky. How he got the money necessary to buy a small little plot of land, I do not know, that was not told me; but he bought a small little plot of land in Ventura County. He wanted to have oil, so he would sleep on the land itself. He didn't build some little shack - he slept right on the ground. With his head to the ground he would hear oil coming in, he would smell oil, and he would come home sometimes in the morning at 6 A.M. and his wife was distraught. "What has happened to you?" He was sleeping on the land bringing it in.

Today the man - I would say he is ten years my senior, which is 68, pushing 70 - he has no financial problems. He has given away fortunes. He is worth over six million, so he told me himself, but now he has another problem, and he has forgotten the name of God. His present problem is boredom. He goes to the track five days a week, Tuesday through Saturday. If he drops ten thousand, it's no problem, if he drops twenty thousand, that's no problem. But he is bored and he is not physically well, and he doesn't remember how he brought oil into being by the name of God. When he put his head on that earth and began to listen, who was listening? If you would say to him: "What are you doing?" "I am smelling oil." That's what he would say. You have called the name of God. "I am smelling oil. I am hearing oil," is what he would say. He brought it all in, but he doesn't remember the name of God.

Now he is saying: "I am unwell." He is blaspheming the name of God. You are told: The man who blasphemes the name of God, stone him to death." The stone is "showing the facts of life," so he is showing the facts of life. "You aren't feeling well, are you?" So you see all the things in the world wrong with him, and you tell him. These are the stones, but he has forgotten and those around him don't know. He once used the name of God wisely and brought wealth into this world. He could bring health into this world if he would use the name of God.

"It is my name forever," said God in Exodus 3. But I will reveal a still greater name as man begins to awaken, and the final name is "Father." And so: "Show us the Father," and you'll be satisfied. "I have been so long with you and yet you do not know me, Phillip? He who has seen me has seen the Father, how then can you say 'show us the Father?'" So here, I tell you, I am the father, and no one knows he is the father. 'Holy Father keep them in thy name, which thou hast given me,' that they may be one even as we are one." There is no way in this world that you and I will know we are one, save through this last act of God revealing himself, when he gives you his last name, which is "Father." I am the Father, that I do know, and you will be the Father of the same and only begotten Son of God. And when you see him, as I have seen him - and you will see him, and you are his Father - then you and I are one. For I can't be the father of your son and not be you. And that is God's final revelation to man on this level.

So, "In many and various ways God spoke of old to our fathers by the prophets, but in these last days he has spoken to us by a Son." And the son reveals the nature of the father. No one knows the father except the son, and anyone to whom the son chooses to reveal him. Until that day comes, use the second revelation - which is forever his name - and use it wisely, as we are told in the 9th *Psalm*, 10th verse: "Those who know thy name trust in thee." If you know the name. The name is the individual himself. God's name is I AM and that is God. So tonight, if you know the name, believe it, trust in his name. And you listen as though you heard what you would hear, were you the man you want to be, and trust in his name, and he will never forsake you.

Here the name changes as man begins to awaken as God, and the final revelation - I know of no greater chapter than the 17th of *John*, where he reveals himself and gives himself to man. "Holy Father glorify me with thine own self." He doesn't want any other glory. It's God himself giving himself to man, for that is his purpose. And when he succeeds in his purpose the man to whom he has given himself is God and God is "Father," the final revelation. Therefore, there must be a child. Where is the child if I am a father? And here comes the child into being and he is David, God's only begotten son. "David, thou art my son, this day I have begotten thee." That is concealed in man until that last moment when the veil is lifted and the fatherhood is revealed to man through the nature of the son. There you see David, and David tells you who you are. You are his father, he calls you father, and calling you father, then the *89th Psalm* is fulfilled: "I have found David" and his cry unto me: "Thou art my father, my God and the Rock of my salvation." And you see him and yet there is no change in your I AM-ness. The self that becomes his father is the same self that it was before, only a far greater self. It includes fatherhood, but the same sense of I AM-ness. You haven't changed your distinct individuality, but now it is enlarged to include fatherhood, and that father is God. And you tell it to the world in the hope you can make it as clear as it is to you.

Whether you accept it or reject it, it is true and the day must come, in time, when each individual will have the same experience and he will pass through it all. Until that happens use his name wisely, as revealed to us through his prophet Moses in the 3rd chapter of Exodus. Use it for wealth, health, or recognition, but don't blaspheme against the name of God. "Unless you believe that I am he you will die in your sins."

So, we are told: "They took up stones to throw at him, because he had offended them, that he had blasphemed the name of God for he claimed 'I am God.'" That was blasphemy on their level and they took up stones to throw at him. What stones? They told him they knew his father. They knew his earthly mother, his brothers, and his sisters, and they named them. They said: I know your father and mother, Joseph and Mary, and they named the four brothers. They implied multiple sisters. And then they began to show him the facts of life, and the facts contradicted his claim. Therefore they were stoning him with the facts of life. These were the stones. Then he disappeared out of their midst. He could not argue with that mind, because they knew exactly his physical background, and he is telling them: "If you will receive what I tell you, I will give you power to become children of God, who were born not of blood, nor of the will of the flesh, nor of the will of man, but of God." This verse is something entirely different in Greek physiology. "To be born of blood" they meant that the seed of man mingled with the blood of woman, and from this union came a child. To be born of the "will of the flesh" is by sexual impulse. It wasn't born that way. To be born of man is to have human parentage. It wasn't born that way. It was born of God. Something entirely different, where man suddenly awakes within himself and he steps out of his own skull to find out that all along he has been sleeping.

Then you read these words in *Revelation 1:18*: "And he thought himself alive and he was dead." Here a man was dead, and all along he believed he was alive. The whole vast world, the sleep is so profound, it is so deep, he doesn't know he is sleeping. And the sleep is so deep he is likened spiritually to a dead man. Then one day, in God's own wonderful time, he awakens himself in man and brings him forth, and then he awakes for the first time to realize all through the ages he has been dead but he didn't know it. But now he is resurrected by the mercy of God. He thought he was asleep while he thought he was awake, and yet he was dead.

In the meanwhile, you who think yourself alive, try this principle by the use of God's name. It will not fail you, I promise you it will not. For one thing bear in mind this: you may have wealth tonight and have it heavily insured - furniture, jewelry, furs, but you left it when you came here tonight, left it wherever you have this outside wealth. You may have stocks and bonds, they may be insured, but you left them wherever they are, maybe in vaults, your homes. Standing here just about two years ago I left this platform and looked out and saw these enormous flames and all these beautiful homes burning. They were all left behind wherever the people were, all consumed in a matter of moments. But one thing you can't leave behind, and you always take it with you after you find the name. Can you go any place where you can leave behind your "I AM"? Where can you go in this world where you will leave behind you the only power in the world, "I AM"? "Those who know thy name put their trust in thee." Not in the bank, not in their social position, their financial, intellectual, or any other position. "Put their trust in thee," Who are you? "I AM." So everyone who came here tonight brought that name with them. When you leave here you are going to take it with you. Maybe you don't know you carried it with you. You can have a treasure and not know you have it. If I had a billion dollars deposited in the bank but I didn't know it, I could die of starvation for want of a dollar; and yet I could sign a check if I knew I had it, and would withdraw it for my earthly need.

You can't leave behind you God's name. He's put himself into you, your very being, your own I AM-ness - that is God. And because it is God, don't blaspheme against the name. Use it wisely, use it lovingly, and I tell you: "What are you hearing?" And you tell me: I am hearing so and so, or I am thinking so and so. Well, see to it that what you are hearing, feeling, what you are thinking, is in harmony with your highest ideal. For you will draw it out just as this man drew out his oil from this little bit of dirt, and today he is worth millions - but bored. You will be able to use it wisely through your earthly days, and maybe in this embodiment the final one will be revealed to you, but only God knows when he reveals the final one.

I can talk about it and tell you about it but I cannot lift the curtain for you -only the son himself can reveal you as the father. I can tell you: you are going to be the father, that I do know, but I have no power to tear that curtain and show you David. He and he alone will reveal you as the father. "No one knows who the son is except anyone to whom the son chooses to reveal him." But I will tell you: one day he is going to tear that curtain from the mind and stand before you and call you father. You will know exactly who he is; there will be no doubt in your mind whatsoever. You are looking at your only begotten son. Begotten not by any woman in this world. Begotten out of your own wonderful being -

your mind, and it's David. And he will be just as he is described in the *Book of Samuel*, no doubt about it.

I can't tell you the thrill that is in store for you after it happens. You are so excited you can't think of anything but. You may bore your friends, you may bore everyone that you meet, because you can't think of anything but this enormous event that has happened to you, this heavenly thing that has taken place. You may be a single man, a man who has never known a woman in this world, but all of a sudden you are a father, and you are a father in the true sense of the word. Then you will know he was "not born of blood, nor of the will of the flesh, nor of the will of man, but of God," and he calls you father, and you know God is his father. He tells you exactly who you are.

Then you have to walk the earth for the remaining years shut out, because you are still wearing the garment of flesh. And although you are now heir to a present and to a promise that has already been fulfilled, you still cannot share it with others, so that it cannot become to you actual or fully realized in you until you take off the garment for the last time. And then you are one with the heavenly host. Everyone is destined - you can't brag about it, you can't crow about it, because you didn't earn it. It was all God's plan from the beginning: "He who began a good work in you" at that moment brought it to completion "at the day of Jesus Christ." And Jesus Christ is God the Father. Therefore, if Jesus Christ is God the Father, and David calls him "Lord," who are you? Are you not then Jesus Christ? Then you realize the words: "Do you not realize that Jesus Christ is in thee, unless of course you fail to meet the test." I hope you realize that we have not failed in our effort.

Eventually you will read the words: And the whole thing disappears, and there was Jesus only. Moses was present, Elijah was present, they all saw the glory of God, and when it all subsided there was Jesus only. For at the name of Jesus Christ every knee will bend and every tongue will confess that he is Lord, the glory of God the Father. It is only Jesus and he has one son and he is sharing his son with you - not walking the street with you as a friend, but as your son. He gives himself to every being in the world, and there is no way he can prove that he actually gave that gift of himself to you, save as David, his only begotten son, as your son. The Bible in miniature is in *John 3:10*. "And God so loved the world he gave his only begotten son." People think he gave his only begotten son and his name is Jesus Christ. No! Jesus Christ by his own confession is God the Father. "You see me Phillip and yet you do not know me. He who has seen me has seen the Father. How then can you say show us the father?"

So the son given could not be that being who calls himself father, and the father is Jesus Christ. Who called him father? David. So he asked the question; nobody asked him. He said: "I am the Father." Then where is the child? So he brings up the question: "What do you think of Christ?" and they said: "The son of David." Then why does David in the spirit call him Lord? If David calls him Lord, how can he be David's son? And no one asked any further questions. David in the spirit calls him "Adonai," a word used by every child when it refers to its father. Every child spoke of its father as "Adonai," translated in the English: "My Lord." So David called him "My father." So he tells you who he is and who David is relative to himself. So David is going to call every being in this world: "my father." And because God is one and his name is one, and at that name every knee must bow, you are destined to know yourself to be Christ Jesus, or God the Father.

But until it is revealed to you, use his name as revealed through his prophet Moses. "And when you go to them just tell them 'I AM' has sent me unto you." Lead them out of the wilderness into light by my name. When you can lead yourself today, no matter where you are, whether you are now bewildered, whether you are unwanted (as you think you are), or unemployed, (as you may be) - lead yourself from these states of barrenness into states of fruition, a fruitful state, in the name. Just simply assume "I AM", and you name it, hear it, smell it, see it to the best of your ability, and to the degree that you remain loyal to what you are imagining and hearing, you will actually externalize it in your world. Don't judge it before you try it.

Now if what I have said this night offends, should it be in conflict with what you believed when you came here, again I go back to Scripture: "And he offended them and then they sold him for thirty pieces of silver." Let me go back into the *Book of Leviticus*. Here we are told: "If an ox gored a slave, male or female, then the owner of the ox must pay to the owner of the slave thirty pieces of silver and then the ox must be stoned." The symbol of Christ is that of an ox. If the Christian doctrine offends, well then he has gored you by whatever he has to say. And now, having gored it, the slave will be censured, that he must be sold for thirty pieces of silver. So, you always fulfill Scripture. The word will always be fulfilled. The prototype of Jesus the Christ was Joseph, and he was sold for twenty pieces of silver. Twenty means "disappointed expectancy." Thirty is divine perfection. Reduce it to a three and three is also associated with resurrection. On the third day the earth rose up out of the deep. So here, if I should offend you by what I say, then make me sorry for my thirty pieces of silver, for Scripture is all about me. For "If the ox gores and in any way hurts a slave" . . . then the ox must be stoned with the facts of life.

People will always throw the bricks at you and remind you of "When they knew you," or even as they know you - for we are all limited as we wear these garments. No man in this world can tell me while he wears the garment that he is not limited. President Kennedy is frightfully limited in his office as President. Bricks are coming all over the place - what he promised in his campaign to get the office, and what he has delivered. And the conflict between what he promised and what he has delivered so far, you could throw all the bricks in the world at him. And he is fully aware of it. You can throw it at the Pope, throw it at the Queen of England, throw it at any person in this world for the lack of getting any ambition of theirs. If I took you into my secret and told you my ambition, and you as a friend know I have not realized it, and you throw at me all the rocks in the world, and remind me of what I told you against what I have accomplished - that is true of every being in the world. Nevertheless, whether you accomplish them or not, go back and apply this principle towards the fulfillment of your dreams.

I can tell you: in my own case, small as it has been, it has all been when I was faithful to the use of God's name. When I dared to assume that I am what at the moment reason denies and my senses deny it, and I remained faithful to it, then I invariably realized it. There have been unnumbered times when I have not been faithful to it. I coasted, as we all coast after a while. Then we are jacked up suddenly and we have to go back to the use of the name. And so, "Those who know thy name put their trust in thee." Not in anything outside of thee. And your name is "I AM," and it is your name forever and forever. So, put your trust in the name of God by walking out of here tonight in the belief that you are already the man, the woman you would like to be and see the world as you would see it, were it true. And to the degree you remain loyal to that assumption, to that degree you will externalize it and reap it as fruit within this world.

Now let us go into the silence.

www.ingramcontent.com/pod-product-compliance
Lightning Source LLC
Chambersburg PA
CBHW020443030426
42337CB00014B/1367